What Can I Be?

STEM Careers from A to Z

Coloring & Activity Book

If you believe it, then you can achieve it!!!
Tiffani Teachey

TIFFANI TEACHEY

Copyright © 2020 by Tiffani Teachey

Written by Tiffani Teachey

Illustrated by Naday Meldova

All rights reserved. No part of this book may be used or reproduced in any manner whatsoever without the prior written permission of the author.

Library of Congress Control Number: 2020924138

ISBN: 978-1-7358289-4-7

Thrive Edge Publishing

*Dedicated to my mother, **Annie Ruth Teachey**, and in loving memory of my father, **Bobby Teachey I**. They instilled in me the value of an education and taught me if you believe it, then you can achieve it! As well as, to my brother, **Bobby Teachey II** who has always lifted me up.*

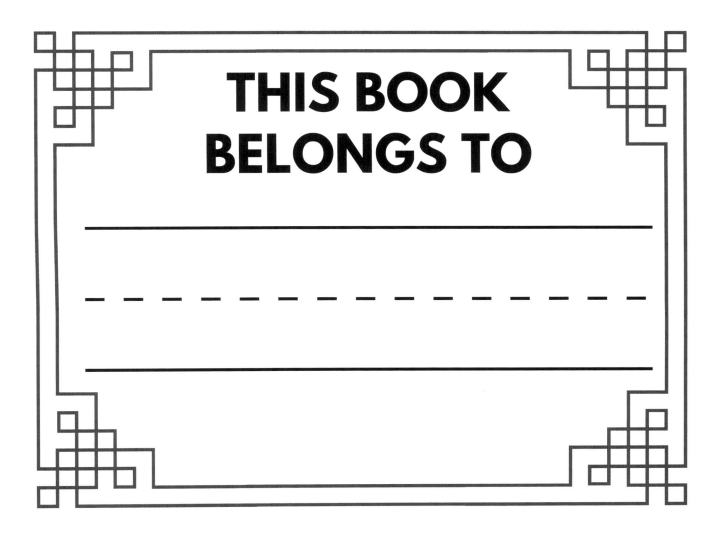

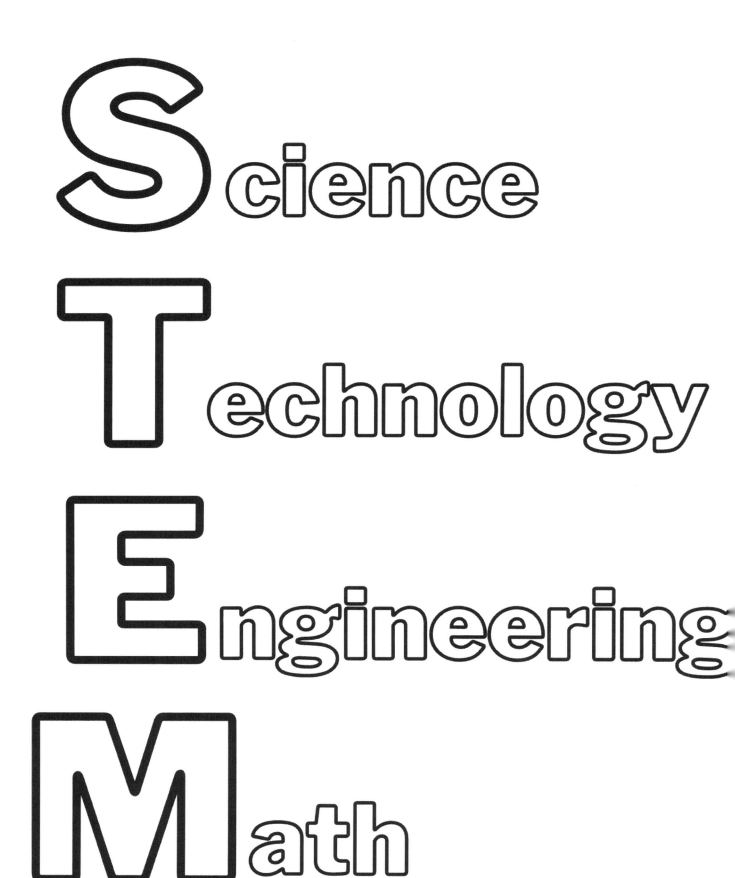

Meet the STEM Crew

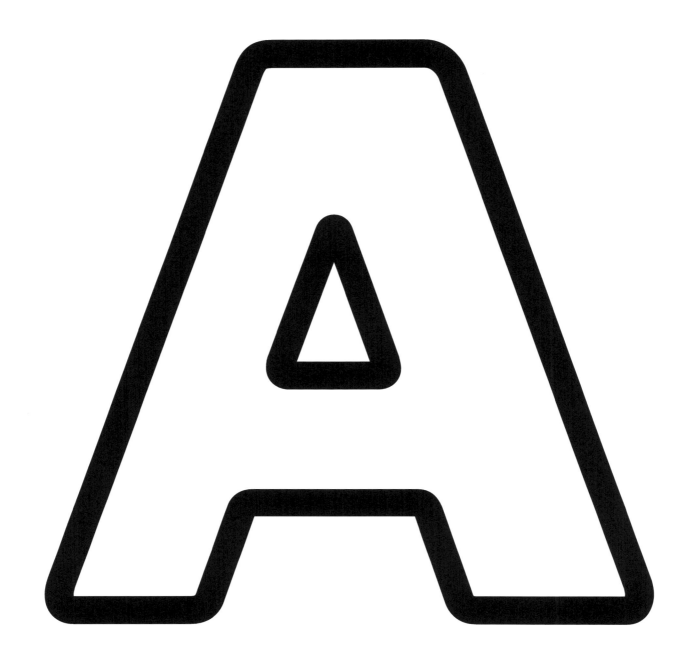

Astronaut

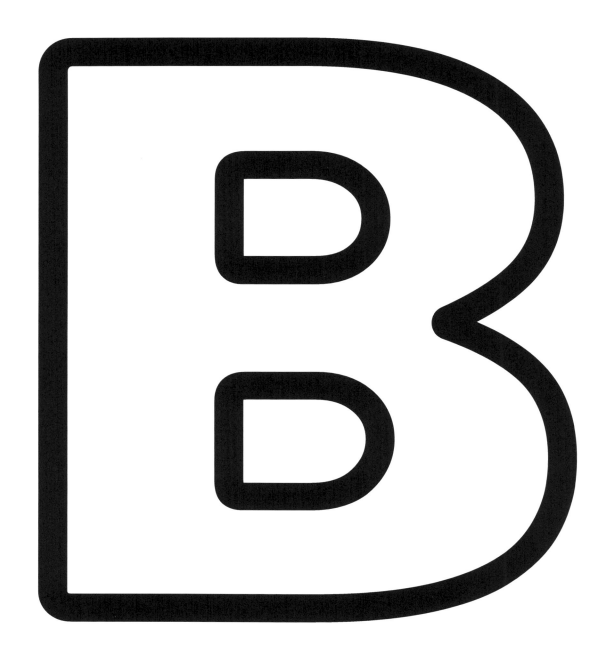

Biologists

| S | | | | | | |

C   E   E
  I   S   N

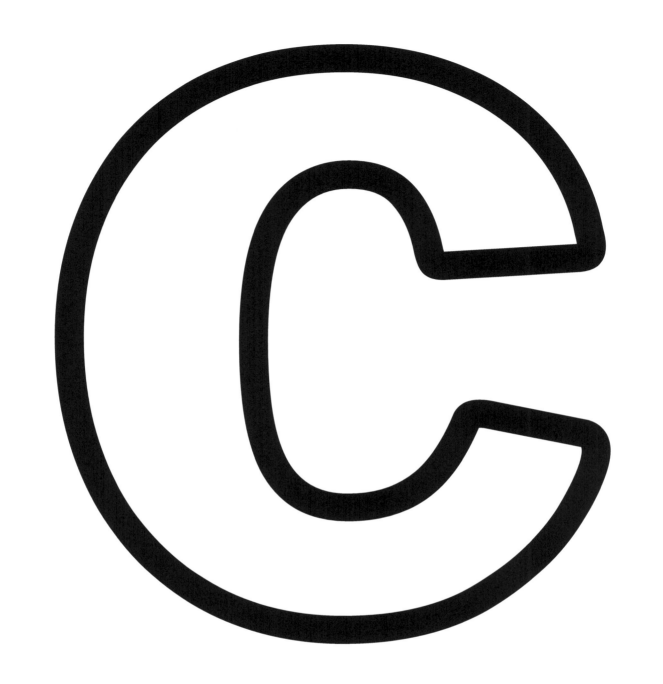

Civil Engineer

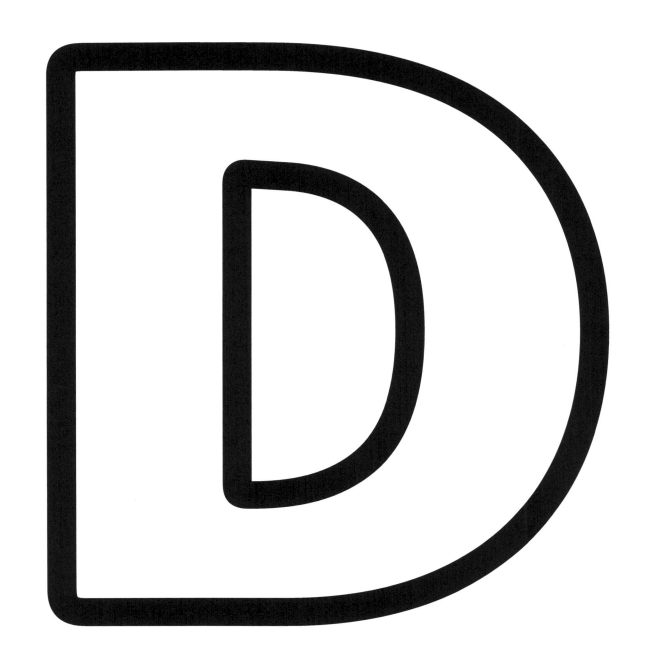

Doctor

Engineering

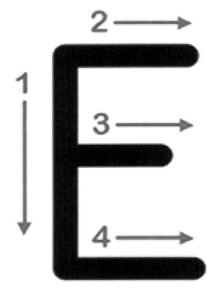
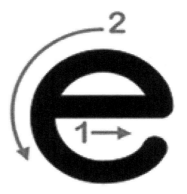
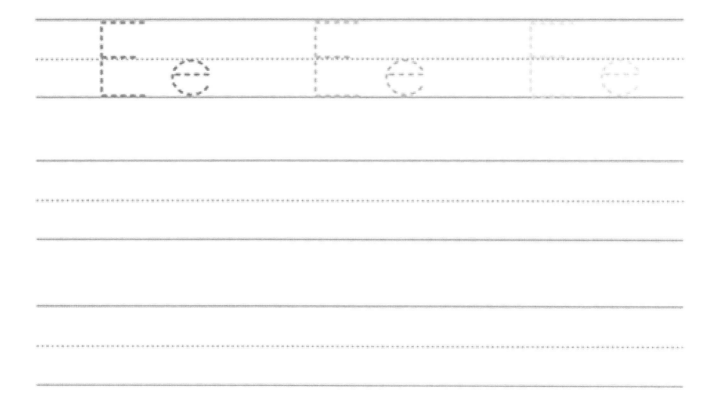

E | | | | | | | | |

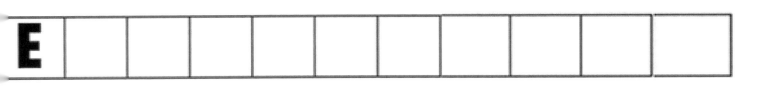

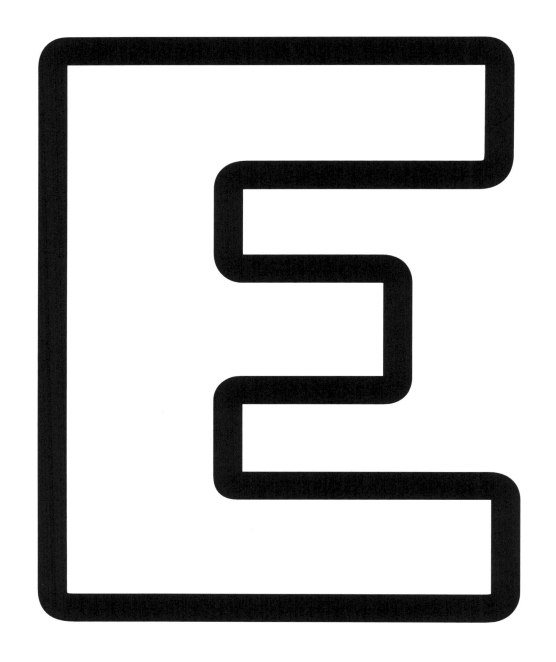

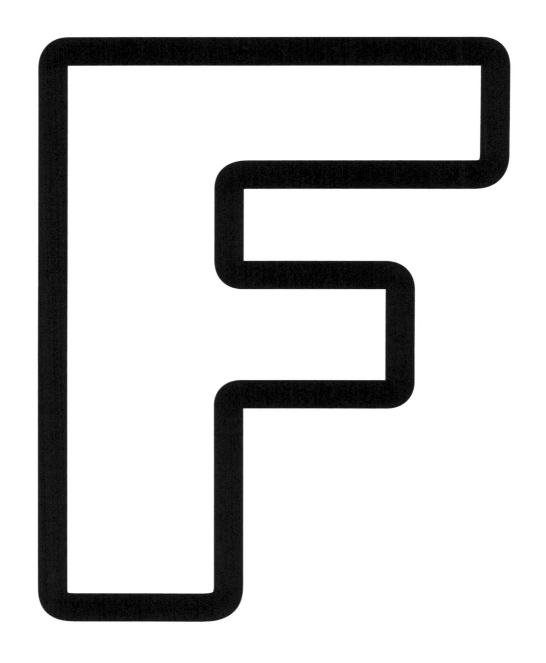

Forester

One

Crossword - Science

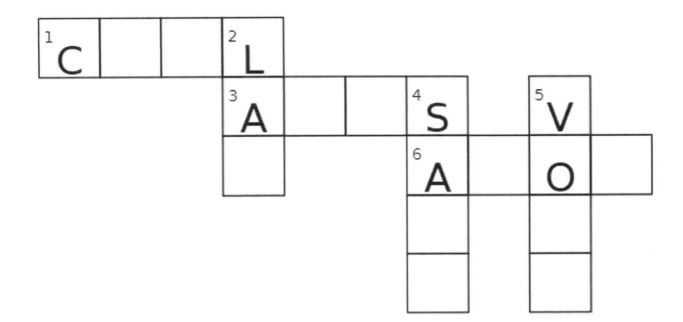

Across
cell
axis
atom

Down
lab
sand
volt

Geologist

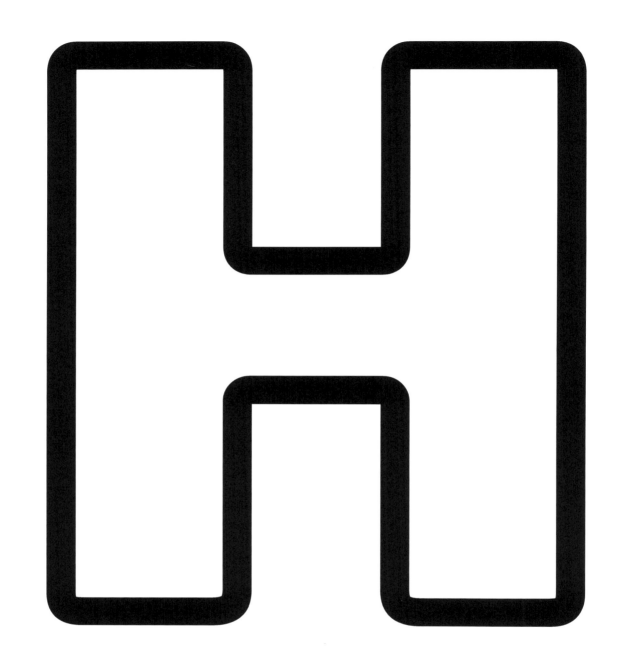

Hydrologist

FIND
6
DIFFERENCES

Information Technologist

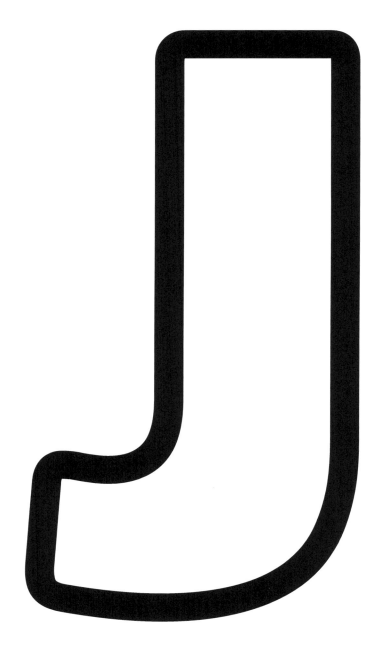

Jet Engineer

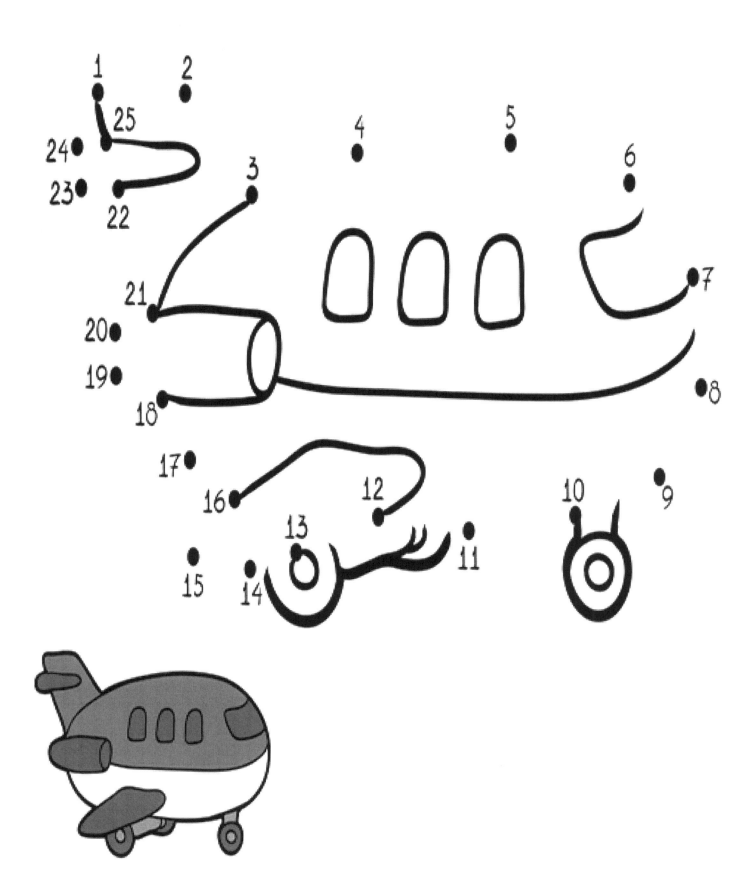

T | | | | | | | | | |

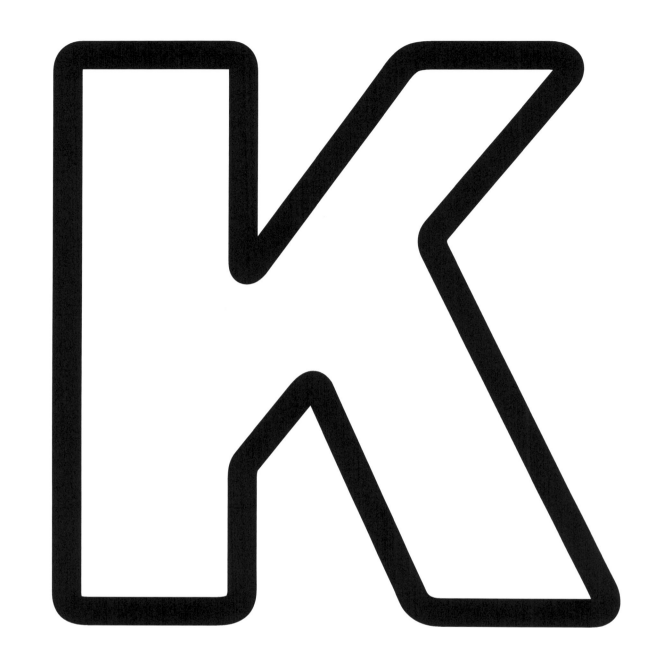

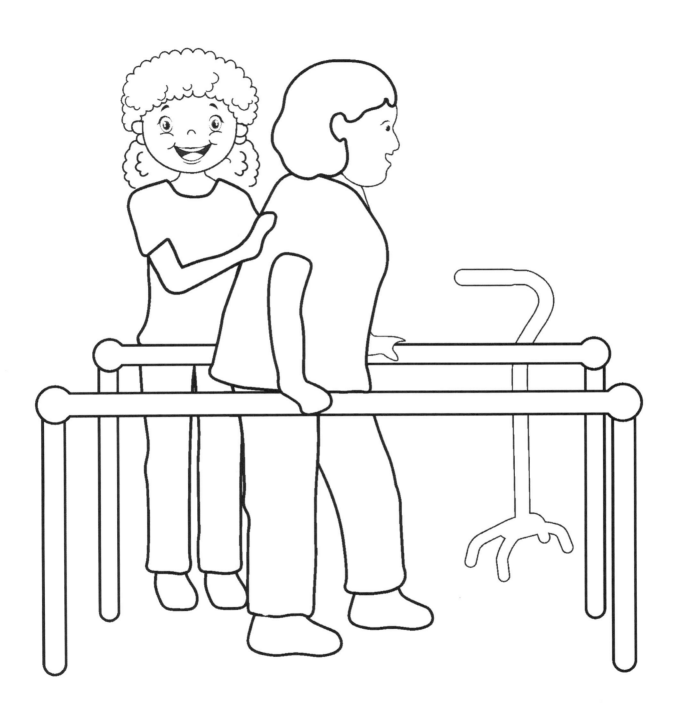

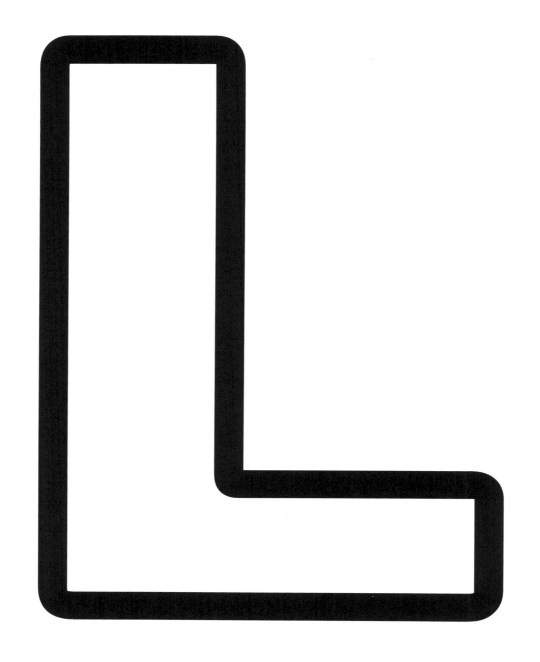

Landscape Architect

Math

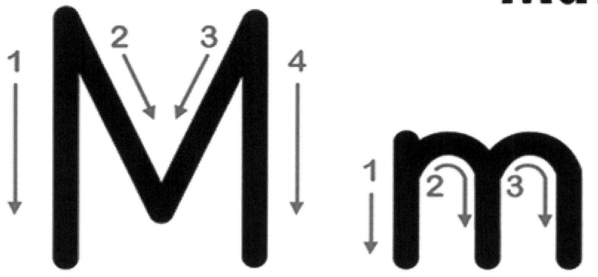

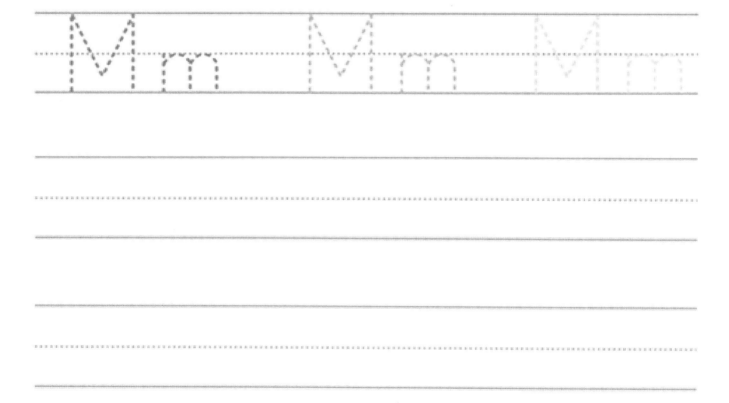

M □ □ □

T   A
 M   H

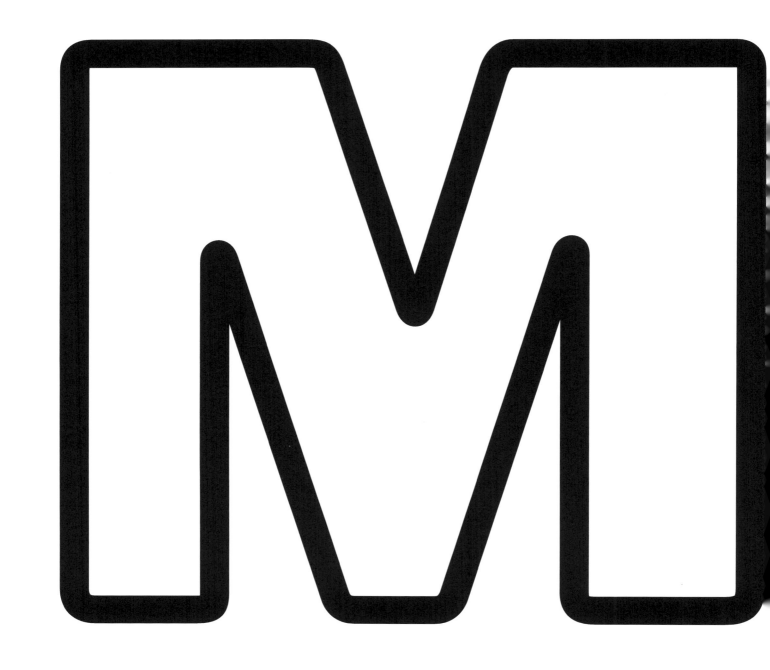

Mechanical Engineer

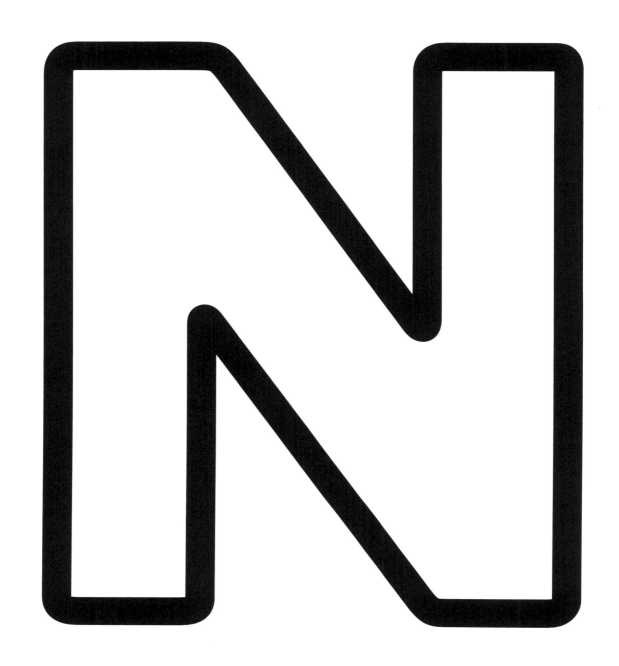

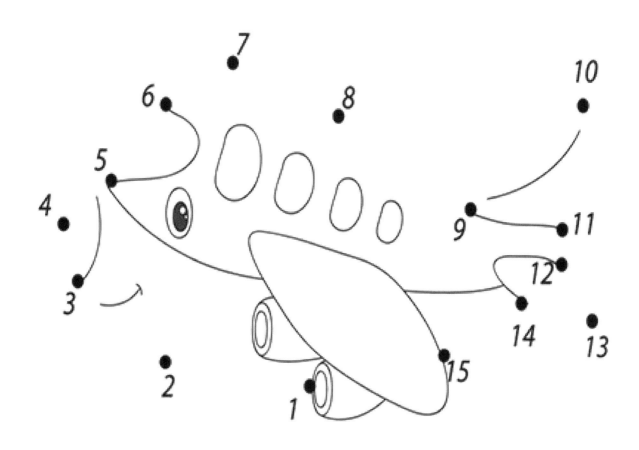

Match the Objects with their Shadow
(Technology)

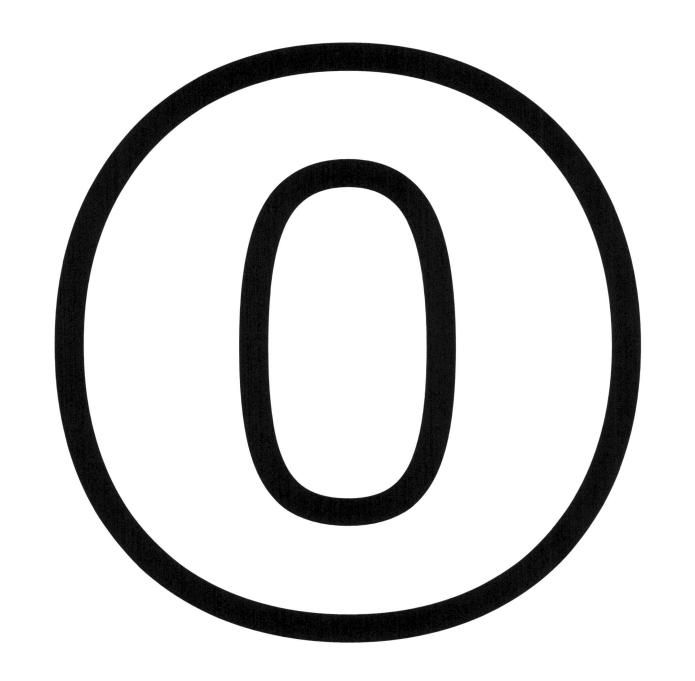

Orthodontist

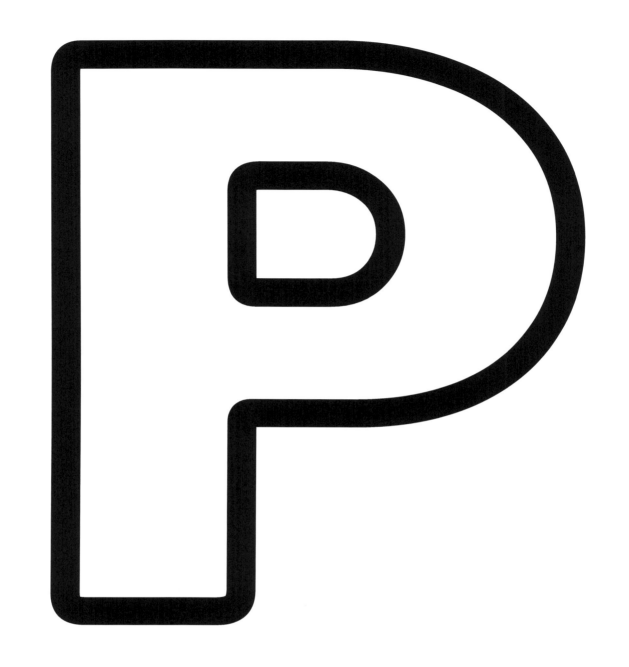

Pediatrician

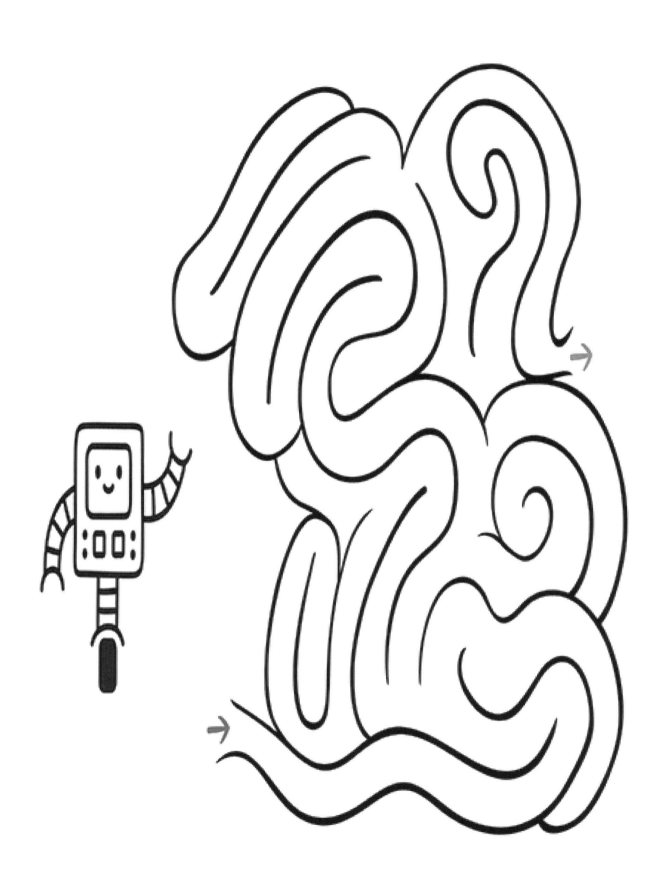

Crossword - Engineering

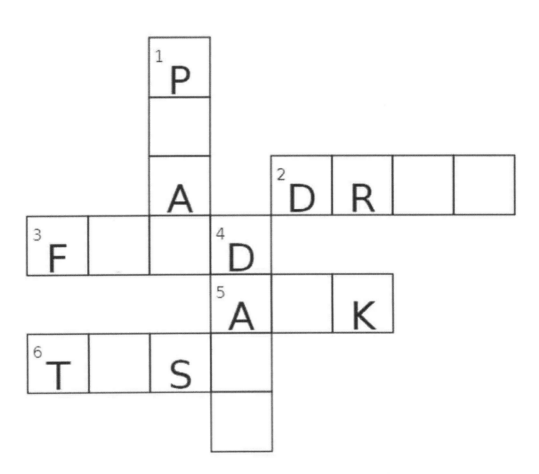

Across

draw
find
ask
test

Down

plan
data

Quality Engineer

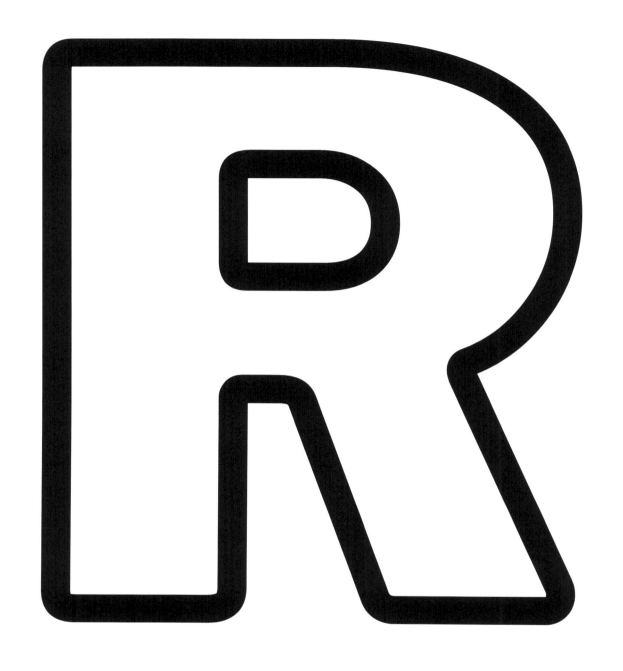

Robotics Engineer

Match the Objects with their Shadow
(Science)

Science

Statistician

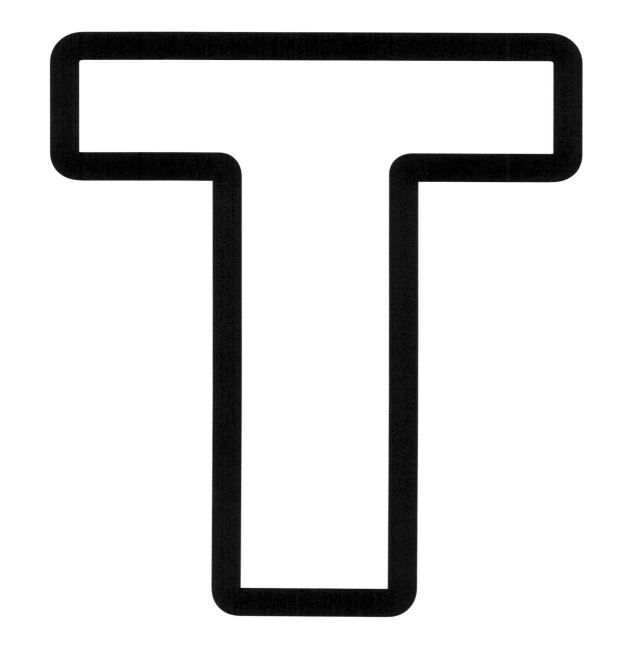

T
Transmission Engineer

Technology

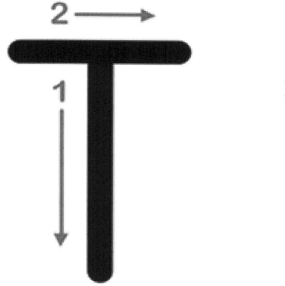

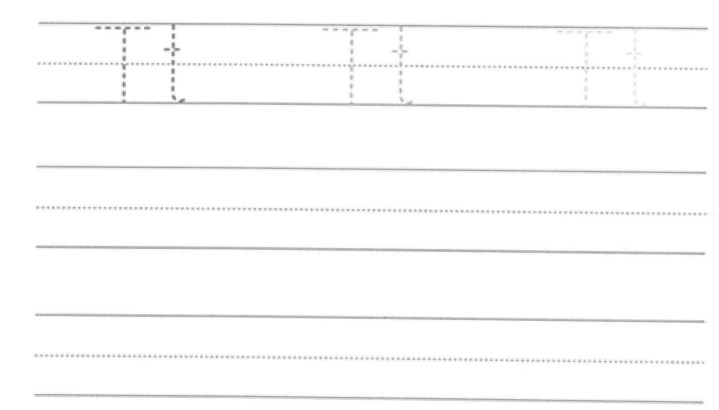

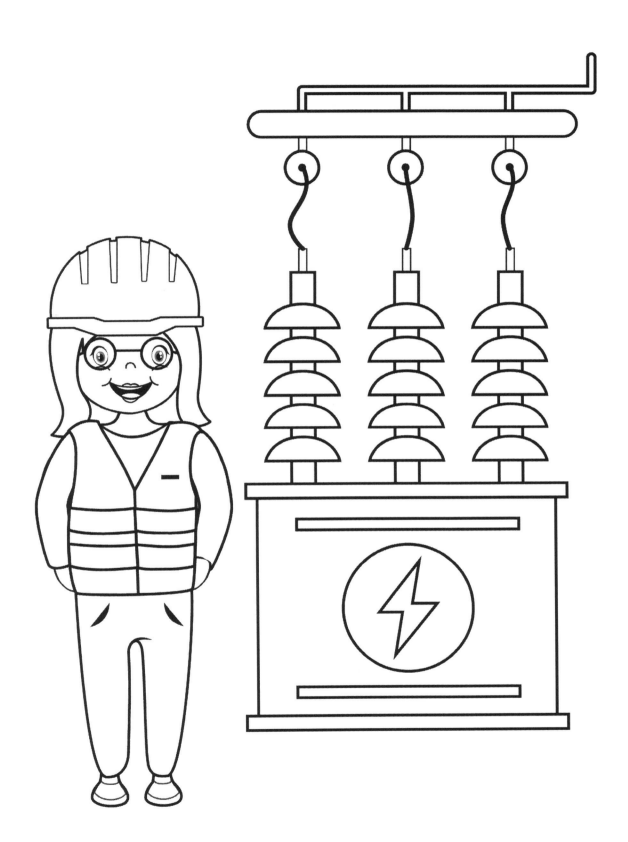

Crossword - Math

Across
one
load
cube

Down
two
zero
line

X-Ray Technician

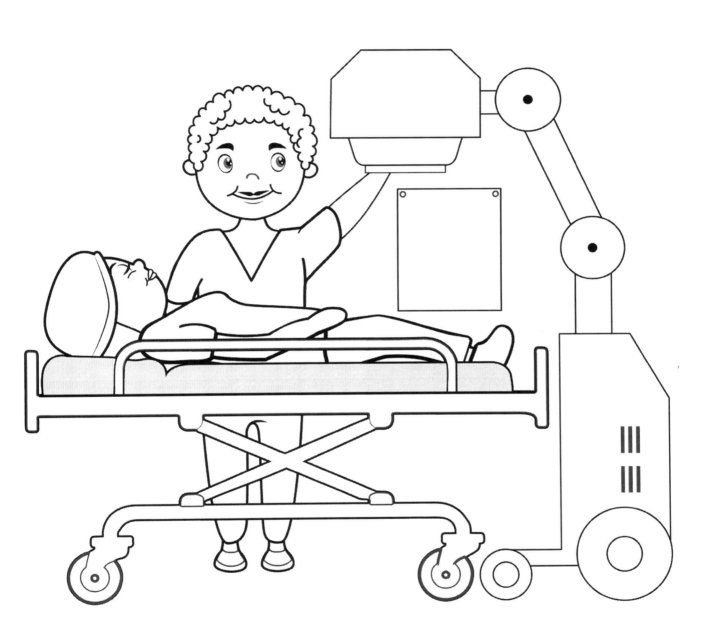

Three

FIND 10 DIFFERENCES

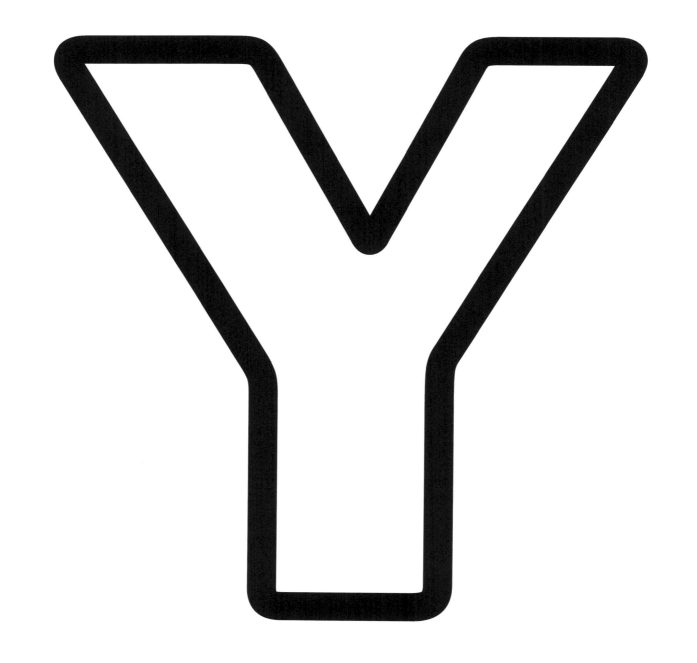

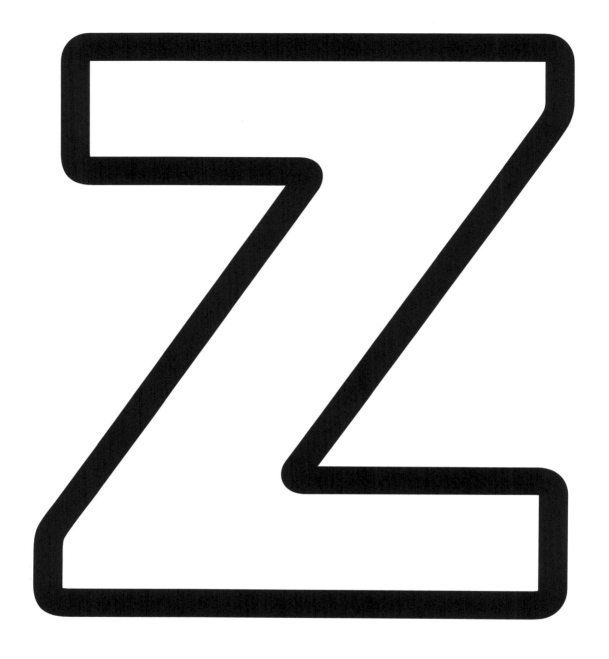

Zoologist

STEM CREW KIDS

Made in the USA
Middletown, DE
23 April 2023

29185225R00049